Hope

'Christians live in the grubbiness and ordinariness of today, but with one foot in the future, glorious beyond words. Too often we fail to connect the two. This short but varied series of devotions helps us to live now in the light of Christ's promises for tomorrow. Each one has helped me to "look forward to the day of God and speed its coming" (2 Peter 3:12).'
Adrian Reynolds, pastor, author, speaker and Head of National Ministries, FIEC

'With a perfect blend of theological rigour, careful exposition, deep insights and pastoral applications, these devotionals are a cut above the rest. They manage to be short and simple, yet packed with thought-provoking truths to stretch you and deepen your walk with the Lord.'
Linda Allcock, author of Deeper Still *and* Head, Heart, Hands

30-DAY DEVOTIONAL

Hope

Edited by Elizabeth McQuoid

INTER-VARSITY PRESS
36 Causton Street, London SW1P 4ST, England
Email: ivp@ivpbooks.com
Website: www.ivpbooks.com

First published 2022

British Library Cataloguing-in-Publication Data
A catalogue record for this book is available from the British Library.

ISBN: 978–1–78974–194–0
eBook ISBN: 978–1–78974–193–3

Set in Avenir 11/15pt
Typeset in Great Britain by CRB Associates, Potterhanworth, Lincolnshire
Printed and bound in Great Britain by Clays Ltd, Elcograf S.p.A.

Printed on paper from sustainable sources.

Inter-Varsity Press publishes Christian books that are true to the Bible and that communicate the gospel, develop discipleship and strengthen the church for its mission in the world.

IVP originated within the Inter-Varsity Fellowship, now the Universities and Colleges Christian Fellowship, a student movement connecting Christian Unions in universities and colleges throughout Great Britain, and a member movement of the International Fellowship of Evangelical Students. Website: www.uccf.org.uk. That historic association is maintained, and all senior IVP staff and committee members subscribe to the UCCF Basis of Faith.

Contributors

Matthew 24:36 – 25:46 and 1 Peter 1:1–12
Don Carson
Don is Research Professor of New Testament at Trinity Evangelical Divinity School in Deerfield, Illinois. He has written more than fifty books, sits on several boards, and is a guest lecturer in academic and church settings around the world. Along with Timothy Keller, he founded The Gospel Coalition.

Romans 8:15–30
Ray Ortlund
Ray is President of Renewal Ministries and a council member of The Gospel Coalition. He has written eight books, including *Marriage and the Mystery of the Gospel.* He was a pastor in California, Oregon and Georgia before founding Immanuel Church in Nashville, Tennessee. Ray now ministers from Immanuel as a pastor to pastors.

2 Corinthians 4:16 – 5:10
Joe Stowell
Joe retired as President of Cornerstone University in Grand Rapids, Michigan, in 2021. From 1987 to 2005, he

was President of Moody Bible Institute in Chicago. He has also been a pastor and is the author of more than twenty books, including *Redefining Leadership: Character-Driven Habits of Effective Leaders.*

1 Thessalonians 4:13–18
Alec Motyer

Alec Motyer was Vice Principal of Clifton Theological College, Bristol, and Vicar of St Luke's Church, Hampstead, before becoming Principal of Trinity College, Bristol. He was much loved on both sides of the Atlantic as a Bible expositor and a prolific author.

Revelation 4:1–11
Paul Mallard

Paul is Senior Pastor of Widcombe Baptist Church in Bath. He was President of the FIEC (Fellowship of Independent Evangelical Churches) and is the author of *Invest Your Suffering, Invest Your Disappointments, Staying Fresh* and *An Identity to Die For.*

Revelation 7:9–12
Jonathan Lamb

Jonathan is Minister-at-Large for Keswick Ministries and Vice President of IFES (International Fellowship of Evangelical Students). He was previously CEO of Keswick Ministries and Director of Langham Preaching. He has written of a number of books, including *Preaching Matters: Encountering the Living God* and *Essentially One: Striving for the Unity God Loves*.

Revelation 21:1–27
Steve Brady
Steve was a pastor in the UK before becoming Principal of Moorlands College, Sopley, Dorset. He has spoken at conferences and conventions around the world, many linked to the UK Keswick Convention, of which he was a trustee and speaker for two decades. He is Senior Pastor at First Baptist Church, Grand Cayman, West Indies.

Revelation 22:1–21
Nigel Lee
Nigel worked with Operation Mobilisation in India, was appointed Head of Student Ministries for UCCF (University and Colleges Christian Fellowship) and was a consultant in evangelism and Bible teaching for the Whitfield Institute. He was a regular contributor to BBC Radio 4's 'Thought for the Day' slot in the *Today* programme.

Preface

What is the collective name for a group of preachers? A troop, a gaggle, a chatter, a pod . . . ? I'm not sure! But in this Food for The Journey series, we have gathered an excellent group of Bible teachers to help us unpack the Scriptures and understand some of the core issues that every Christian needs to know.

Each book is based on a particular theme and contains excerpts from messages given by much loved Keswick Convention speakers, past and present. When necessary, the language has been updated but, on the whole, this is what you would have heard had you been listening in the tent on Skiddaw Street. A wide, though not exhaustive, selection of Bible passages explores the key theme, and each day of the devotional ends with a fresh section on how to apply God's Word to your own life and situation.

Whether you are a Convention regular or have never been to Keswick, this Food for the Journey series provides a unique opportunity to study the Scriptures and a particular topic with a range of gifted Bible teachers by your side. Each book is designed to fit in your jacket pocket or handbag, so that you can read it anywhere – over the breakfast table, on the commute into work or college, while you are waiting in your car, during your lunch break or in bed at night. Wherever life's journey takes you, time in God's Word is vital nourishment for your spiritual walk.

Our prayer is that these devotionals become your daily feast, a nourishing opportunity to meet with God through his Word. Read, meditate on, apply and pray through the Scriptures given for each day, and allow God's truths to take root and transform your life.

If these devotionals whet your appetite for more, there is a 'For further study' section at the end of each book. You can also visit our website <www.keswickministries.org/resources> to find the full range of books, study guides, CDs, DVDs and mp3s available.

Let the word of Christ dwell in you richly.
(Colossians 3:16, ESV)

Introduction
Real hope

Punishing hours in the gym. Hail, rain and mucky pitches. Strict diets and injury.

That's been my son's life for the past few years. His goal? To play rugby for the Welsh national team.

Despite my inability to master the finer points of the game, I and my husband have valiantly cheered him on from the wet, windy sidelines of various northern pitches. From front-row seats, we've watched his tentative dream turn into a tangible hope.

But nail-bitingly close to that dream being realized, just when success was looming ever closer . . . a pandemic struck. Our hope deflated quicker than a punctured ball, with all the uncertainty and pit-in-the-stomach disappointment.

That's our story. You will have yours. Most of us know all too well that rollercoaster of emotions.

As you read this, you may well be hoping for a holiday in the sun, to welcome a new baby into your life, for your children to thrive, or for health problems to end and your retirement to be long.

We are hard-wired to hope. But when hope is dashed or our expectations are not met, it's easy to despair. And even when our hopes *are* realized, let's face it, we're not satisfied for long and, before we know it, we're hoping for something newer, bigger and even better. And on we go.

God *does* have something far bigger and better planned for us. Earth-bound hope ultimately leads to futility, but God's hope is eternal, guaranteed and glorious. It is more than knowing that we will go to heaven when we die. The moment a believer breathes his or her last, the Christian's spirit is immediately transported into the presence of Christ; as Paul says, we are 'away from the body and at home with the Lord' (2 Corinthians 5:8). But this is just an intermediate state, for being in heaven is not the end of the story. One day Jesus will return, the whole cosmos will be renewed, and believers who have been in heaven and those believers still living will be changed into the likeness of Christ and given resurrection bodies. God will come down to live with his people in the new heaven and new earth. How wonderful is that!

Life with Christ in this eternal kingdom is 'the hope set before us' (Hebrews 6:18). We can cling to it in dark days, for it's a hope we can literally stake our lives on. Why? Because Jesus is already in God's presence and he is praying us home. He offered himself as the perfect sacrifice for sin and then ascended into heaven, where he anchors our salvation, securing it for ever. Jesus' death and resurrection blaze a trail for us and represent the guarantee that we, too, will be raised to new life (Hebrews 6:19–20).

So, what are we to do while we wait? Prepare for God's kingdom to come on earth as it is in heaven, endeavouring to bring new creation values into every sphere of life. God tells us about the future not so that we can nit-pick over details or speculate about the timing of Jesus' return, but to give us hope. We can enjoy the pleasures of earth, knowing that they point to the far greater delights we'll experience in the presence of God. We can even endure suffering because we know God is – and always will be – on the throne and in control. Our earthly sorrows pale by comparison with the glory that awaits us. In the meantime, God can use them to refine our character and make us more like Jesus. These sorrows help to detach us from this world and increase our longing for the next one.

The new heaven and new earth will mean no more tears, pain or worry, but that will be nothing compared to the joy of being in Jesus' presence for ever – not only worshipping him but also reigning with him. We can place all our hopes for life and death on 'Christ Jesus our hope' (1 Timothy 1:1).

In fact, he's the only safe place to put our hope: he'll never disappoint us, never stop loving us, never leave us and never stop working within us. He will guard and keep our hope in this life and be our joy throughout eternity.

This devotional is not designed to answer every question we might have about the future but, by looking at selected Bible passages, we will find our appetites whetted for what God has planned and a sense of hope firmly instilled within us. From 1 Thessalonians, we gain assurance about what happens to believers who die before Christ's second coming. Matthew and 2 Corinthians tell us how to live as we wait for Christ's return. Through studying 1 Peter, we remember that Jesus' resurrection guarantees our eternal inheritance. Romans looks forward to the return of Christ, which will bring an end to suffering and the renewal of the whole creation, and Revelation describes God's presence with us in the new heaven and new earth.

It's not wrong to hope for holidays, good health or for your children to flourish – or even for a place on the rugby team. God has given us these things as gifts to enjoy. But there is so much more to look forward to. The 'hope set before us' is far bigger than we could ever imagine.

This devotional invites you to discover the glorious future God has planned, and to be filled with immeasurable and inexhaustible hope.

> May the God of hope fill you with all joy and peace as you trust in him, so that you may overflow with hope by the power of the Holy Spirit.
> (Romans 15:13)

Matthew

The tax collector who left his work to follow Jesus wrote this Gospel (see Matthew 9:9–13). Although it appears first in the New Testament order, it was not the earliest Gospel to be written. Matthew drew from Mark's Gospel, but arranged his material around five of Jesus' sermons: the Sermon on the Mount (chapters 5 – 7); the commissioning of the twelve disciples (chapter 10); the parables of the kingdom (chapter 13); church life and discipleship (chapter 18); and judgment and the end of the world (chapters 23 – 25). Matthew emphasized that Jesus was the Messiah predicted in the Old Testament who would one day return. He urged his readers to be ready for this final day by repenting of sin and pursuing whole-life discipleship.

Day 1

Read Matthew 24:36 – 25:46
Key verses: Matthew 24:37–39

....

³⁷ As it was in the days of Noah, so it will be at the coming of the Son of Man. ³⁸ For in the days before the flood, people were eating and drinking, marrying and giving in marriage, up to the day Noah entered the ark; ³⁹ and they knew nothing about what would happen until the flood came and took them all away. That is how it will be at the coming of the Son of Man.

What does the Bible teach about the context of Jesus' second coming?

Jesus says it will be like 'the days of Noah' (verse 37). The parallel he draws is not with the wickedness but with the normality of the times. People in Noah's day were not transcendently more wicked than any other group in the history of the world. So, in the days before Jesus returns, people will go to the pub for a drink; they'll marry; they'll give their daughters in marriage. In other words, the Son of Man will come the way the flood came: unexpectedly, to all but those who are waiting for it.

The other vignettes are similar. In the ancient world you ground your flour, either with large millstones dragged around by oxen or small hand mills, usually controlled by two women. Typically, those women would be sisters or a mother and a daughter – family members. When Christ comes, one will be taken and the other left behind. Whether this means individuals are taken and transported to glory or taken in judgment doesn't make any difference. The point is about the absolute separation of people whom you would think, because of family ties, should be together. But one will be ready for the Master's return and the other will not (verse 41). In the same way, two will be working in the field – in the nature of first-century farming, probably a father and son or two brothers, or similar – and, again, one will be taken and the other left behind (verse 40).

Then (in verses 43–44) we're given the most startling image that keeps recurring in the New Testament: Jesus will come like a thief in the night. The point here is the unexpectedness, not the immorality, of the theft.

The message from these three scenes is that because we don't know when the Lord Jesus is coming back, we must make sure we're ready. If we don't want to be surprised at his return, we need to be waiting expectantly.

As we wait for Christ's return, it is easy to become complacent, living comfortably in our fallen world, enjoying its pleasures, consumed with routines and responsibilities. Our lives can look almost indistinguishable from those of the unbelievers around us. Ask yourself, 'If Jesus came back today, would I be surprised, ashamed or delighted?' Pray through your day – about your work and conversations, the money you'll spend and the people you'll serve. Think and act in such a way that you are always ready for the Lord's return. His return is not unexpected, so let's make sure we're not surprised when it happens.

Day 2

Read Matthew 24:36 – 25:46
Key verses: Matthew 24:45–47

....

[45] *'Who then is the faithful and wise servant, whom the master has put in charge of the servants in his household to give them their food at the proper time?* [46] *It will be good for that servant whose master finds him doing so when he returns.* [47] *Truly I tell you, he will put him in charge of all his possessions.*

How should we wait?

A pattern that immediately emerges from this parable, and repeats itself throughout the rest of chapters 24 and 25, is that each fresh parable picks up on one or more themes from the previous material. Verses 36–44 emphasize the unexpectedness of Christ's coming; so here, too, in verses 45–51, the wicked servant discovers the master returning at a moment when he does not expect him. It picks up the previous theme, but it adds something else – it enriches the notion of *how* we are to wait for the

Master's return: we are to wait for the Lord Jesus as stewards who must give an account of their service, faithful or otherwise.

The judgment pictured here is not reserved for utter outsiders (pagans) but for people who seem to be the Master's faithful slaves: those who view themselves as his stewards but forget that *they must give an account*. These are nominal Christian leaders who, instead of feeding the sheep, are exploiting them; instead of nurturing and building up the flock of God, they are fleecing the animals and eating the mutton. And they must give an account.

Many clergy will fall under this judgment. And not just clergy – doesn't James warn us that not many of us should be teachers, knowing that we shall face stricter judgment (James 3:1–2)? We put Christian leaders into places of authority, and sometimes they become so egocentric that this authority is more important to them than faithfulness to the Master. We got rid of the pope and then generated our own popes. It's not that these leaders are saved by good works; that's not the point at all. Rather, if they really are the Master's, they will live and serve in a certain kind of way. If they are really not the Master's, they will view whatever position of authority they have been assigned as a perk for themselves, and use their gifts, leadership and office to push down, hurt and exploit others.

This parable reminds us that we must wait for the Lord's return like stewards who must give account of their service. Like the good servant, we are to be prepared for the Lord to come at any time. If we are faithful throughout the long delay, we will be highly rewarded at the end (verses 45–47). In contrast, unfaithful servants will face judgment, where there is gnashing of teeth (verses 48–51).

Jesus' return will be a day of reckoning, when the worth of our service will be examined. Knowing we are to give an account, the only way to be prepared is to live faithfully now. Today, ask God to help you to be a good steward of the money, time, responsibilities, gifts, roles and relationships he has entrusted to you.

The world asks, 'What does a man own?'
Christ asks, 'How does he use it?'
(Andrew Murray, a nineteenth-century pastor)

Day 3

Read Matthew 24:36 – 25:46
Key verses: Matthew 25:1–5

....

> ¹*At that time the kingdom of heaven will be like ten virgins who took their lamps and went out to meet the bridegroom.* ²*Five of them were foolish and five were wise.* ³*The foolish ones took their lamps but did not take any oil with them.* ⁴*The wise ones, however, took oil in jars along with their lamps.* ⁵*The bridegroom was a long time in coming, and they all became drowsy and fell asleep.*

What happens when the bridegroom is delayed?

In the first century, weddings started with the groom meeting the bride and her family for some celebrations. Then, at some point, there would be a procession through the street and everybody else who was invited to the real celebration would join in. Knowing that time could slip by, these guests would be waiting on the route with their torches ready, signifying that they were part of the invited group. Together, they would process down to the groom's place where the celebrations would continue. The torches they held were passes to get into the party. Then the gates were shut and the wedding festivities proper began.

In this parable, five virgins who are waiting along the way have enough oil for their lamps to burn, but they don't have any additional oil if it runs out. The five others are wise, prepared for a long delay. When suddenly the cry goes up, 'Here's the bridegroom!', those with their lamps flickering out run into town to find more oil. When they return to the street, everybody has gone. Finally, they get to the party: 'We belong here, too!' they cry. But they just look like gatecrashers. If they really did belong, surely they would have been waiting? That's the way the culture works. They weren't waiting for the groom; they were off doing something else. So they are excluded.

The Master's coming may be long delayed. This is important for many reasons. At the lowest level, it should engender within us perseverance. At a slightly higher level, it should engender a sense of strategy. What do we do about training the next generation? What do we do about mentoring? How do we ensure that our children have learned biblical truths and are living them out? We begin to think about writing books and courses, building projects and other trajectories – all because we realize that the Lord could be long delayed.

It is part of our Christian responsibility to think not only 'Could it be today, Lord?' but also, assuming that it's not, 'How can I give, plan, pray and serve, so that I'm showing by the way I live that I, too, recognize that the Lord's return could be long delayed?'

If you knew that Jesus was not going to come back in your lifetime, what difference would it make to your priorities and prayers?

If the Lord Jehovah makes us wait, let us do so with our whole hearts; for blessed are all they that wait for Him. He is worth waiting for. The waiting itself is beneficial to us: it tries faith, exercises patience, trains submission, and endears the blessing when it comes. The Lord's people have always been a waiting people.
(C. H. Spurgeon, *The Treasury of David*, Psalm 130:5, <https://archive.spurgeon.org/treasury/ps130.php>)

Day 4

Read Matthew 24:36 – 25:46
Key verses: Matthew 25:19–21

....

19 *After a long time the master of those servants returned and settled accounts with them.* 20 *The man who had received five bags of gold brought the other five. 'Master,' he said, 'you entrusted me with five bags of gold. See, I have gained five more.'*

21 *His master replied, 'Well done, good and faithful servant! You have been faithful with a few things; I will put you in charge of many things. Come and share your master's happiness!'*

Who will hear the words, 'Well done, good and faithful servant'?

Jesus tells the parable of a master who assigned money to his slaves (the Greek word *doulos*, translated as 'servant', actually means 'slave'), according to their ability and character, and then went off on a long journey.

Now, slavery in the ancient world was very different from later practice. People became slaves for different reasons, such as personal bankruptcy, and exercised different levels of responsibility. Some were badly treated but others were accountants in family businesses, for example.

The slave who had received five bags put his money to work. Perhaps he bought a boat and started a fishing business, or a farm and started to work it? When the master returned and wanted the accounts settled, the slave sold everything off and brought in the bags of gold. Instead of five bags, there were now ten: he'd doubled it – a 100% return!

Similarly, for the slave with two bags of gold: he'd worked faithfully according to his ability and doubled his money as well. The master said to both, 'You have been faithful with a few things; I will put you in charge of many things. Come and share your master's happiness!'

Here's a glimpse of eternity. You are not going to sit around on a puffy cloud playing a harp. You're going to have fantastic responsibilities, and the Master will give you the gifts and graces to take care of them. Even more, you will enter into your Master's happiness. When the earthly master comes back, he is supposed to be served by slaves who ensure that *he* is happy. But this Master ensures that all the *slaves* are happy with the same happiness that he has. In the new heaven and the new earth, the happiness of Jesus himself will be given to those who are only slaves!

We might be sympathetic towards the third man. If he is successful, none of the result will be his; it's owned by his master. If he loses the capital, what would the master say? In the master's response, Jesus is not justifying slavery any more than he was justifying theft in Matthew 24:43. It's an analogy. His point is that the slave *owes* his master something, just as you and I are slaves of Christ. In the New Testament, this image is continually used to depict what our true discipleship to Jesus looks like. We have been bought for a price. We are no longer our own; we owe him everything and everything is his.

While we wait for Jesus' return, we are to improve the Master's assets by living lives of obedience, mentoring others, bearing witness to Jesus, and using the gifts, graces and money that God has given to us. Today, ask yourself, 'Given that I am Christ's, that all that I've got is Christ's, that whatever abilities or resources I have are all Christ's, what am I doing with what's entrusted to me in order to improve the Master's assets?'

Day 5

Read Matthew 24:36 – 25:46

Key verses: Matthew 25:34–36

....

34 Then the King will say to those on his right, 'Come, you who are blessed by my Father; take your inheritance, the kingdom prepared for you since the creation of the world. 35 For I was hungry and you gave me something to eat, I was thirsty and you gave me something to drink, I was a stranger and you invited me in, 36 I needed clothes and you clothed me, I was ill and you looked after me, I was in prison and you came to visit me.'

The stakes are high. When Christ returns, the ultimate division will take place: those who go into eternal life and those who go into eternal punishment.

But this parable is not teaching that if you're kind to a homeless person or you work for an organization that helps prisoners, you are doing it unto Jesus and he will look favourably on you on the last day. Jesus refers to those to be helped as 'the least of these brothers and sisters of mine' (25:40). We want to extend that to everybody who is poor, but that's simply not what the expression means. It certainly never means it in Matthew. Jesus' 'brothers' refers to his half-brothers through Mary or, if the word is used in any sort of metaphorical sense, invariably it refers to his disciples (Matthew 12:48–49 or 28:10).

Besides, if you serve others so that Jesus will welcome you into eternity, surely you'd be expecting him to notice your endeavours? But both the sheep and goats are surprised. When individuals helped the least in the kingdom, they didn't do so thinking, 'Oh, I'm doing this for Jesus' sake.' They did it because they were brothers and sisters in Christ, part of that community.

Do you see how closely this ties in with a massive theme in the New Testament: how Jesus identifies with his church? When Jesus appears to Saul on the road to Damascus, he doesn't say, 'Why are you persecuting my church?' No. He says, 'Why are you persecuting *me*? For inasmuch as you do it to the least of these of my brothers and sisters you are doing it unto me' (see Acts 9:4 and Matthew 25:40). Christians, because they have been transformed by grace, form a network; they constitute the church, the people of the living God. So they will care for one another. When Christians go into prison, they will look after them. When believers are starving elsewhere, they will send money, not to earn Brownie points but because they are part of the redeemed family of God. We are to wait for Christ's return as people whose lives are so transformed by the gospel that we unselfconsciously serve our brothers and sisters in Christ.

What importance Christ places on the church! He never intended the wait for his return to be a solitary experience. Let's love and pray for one another so that care becomes instinctive. Be so transformed by gospel truths that serving one another is the natural overflow. And may our devotion to one another point people to Christ, so that they, too, will be ready for his coming.

Romans

The great reformer Martin Luther described the book of Romans as 'the chief part of the New Testament and the very purest Gospel'.[1] It is packed with key theological truths, which the apostle Paul lived and died by. It was probably written during his third missionary journey, on the way back to Jerusalem with the collection he'd received for the poverty-stricken believers. Paul is at pains to convey the full scope of God's glorious salvation plan and the future glory awaiting the whole of creation, including us. To this mixed congregation, which had never had a visit from an apostle, Paul carefully sets out the basic truths of the gospel and God's redemption plan for both Jews and Gentiles, almost like a theological essay. He explains why Christians can be confident of God's love, certain that God will conform them to the likeness of Christ, secure in their salvation and in the hope of final glory.

---

1   Martin Luther, *Commentary on Romans*, J. Theodore Mueller (trans.), Kregel Publications, 2003, p. xiii.

Day 6

Read Romans 8:15–30
Key verses: Romans 8:17–18

....

> ¹⁷ Now if we are children, then we are heirs – heirs of God and co-heirs with Christ, if indeed we share in his sufferings in order that we may also share in his glory. ¹⁸ I consider that our present sufferings are not worth comparing with the glory that will be revealed in us.

Is following Jesus worth all the sacrifice and suffering?

The apostle Paul has 'considered' (verse 18) this question and concluded that, compared with the weight of glory to come, our sufferings now don't even register on the scales.

Paul is not minimizing our suffering. His point, in verse 17, is that we don't just suffer for Christ; we suffer with him. Following Jesus is hard; each day, we take up our crosses (Luke 9:23). But suffering with him means he goes with us as our faithful Friend. The pain you feel, he feels and he bears.

But, more than this, the Bible promises that our present sufferings are not robbing us of our happiness; they are achieving for us 'an eternal weight of glory' (2 Corinthians 4:17, ESV) – our own personal gravitas. We hate being trivialized; we long to stand tall with dignity. God created us for it. So don't be embarrassed by your longing; it is of God. But this existence we're stuck with right now *cannot* satisfy us. This life is good. But it is good the way air is good. I enjoy breathing. But when I'm hungry, air cannot satisfy, no matter how much I inhale. We are hungry for the weight of glory here in a world of breezy air. And God promises to satisfy our glory-hunger.

The author and philosopher Peter Kreeft explains what our future glory is worth now:

> Suppose both death and hell were utterly defeated. Suppose the fight was fixed. Suppose God took you on a crystal ball trip into your future and you saw that despite everything – your sin, your smallness, your stupidity – you could have free for the asking your whole crazy heart's deepest desire: heaven, eternal joy. Would you not return fearless and singing? What can earth do to you, if you are guaranteed Heaven? To fear the worst earthly loss would

be like a millionaire fearing the loss of a penny – less, a scratch on a penny.

(Peter Kreeft, *Heaven*, Ignatius Press, 1989, p. 183)

This is why we keep on walking with the Lord, no matter what the cost is here and now.

Our suffering, sadness and grief often feel raw and overwhelming but, in the light of the glory that will be ours one day, they are like a mere scratch on a penny. Today, keep that image in mind as you persevere in the faith, loving Christ and living for him. Hold on to the hope of future glory, remembering that Christ knows about your suffering. He loves you, is with you and is praying for you.

How did Paul handle his sufferings and encourage the church to face theirs? Not by trying to produce heaven on earth, but by recognizing that for the Christian the best is yet to be. He took the moment and put it in the larger context of God's unfolding purpose, not only for time but also in eternity.

(Alistair Begg, *Made for His Pleasure*, Moody Press, 1996, p. 116)

Day 7

Read Romans 8:15–30
Key verses: Romans 8:19–21

....

¹⁹For the creation waits in eager expectation for the children of God to be revealed. ²⁰For the creation was subjected to frustration, not by its own choice, but by the will of the one who subjected it, in hope ²¹that the creation itself will be liberated from its bondage to decay and brought into the freedom and glory of the children of God.

What are you longing for?

Creation is longing for the 'children of God to be revealed'. J. B. Phillips puts it another way: 'The whole creation is on tiptoe to see the wonderful sight of the sons of God coming into their own.' We ruined everything in the Garden of Eden when we disobeyed God. But his remedy is not a blind natural process. God himself reversed the decline through the second Adam, Jesus, the perfect man. And, right now, the creation longs for the day when we all will be made royal again, trustworthy again, like the risen Jesus. That Greek word translated 'eager expectation' suggests someone craning his or her neck to see what's coming: 'the children of God to be revealed'. That's us – along with millions and millions of other ordinary stumblers who have found their future in stumbling towards Jesus. On that great and final day when the whole universe is renewed, God will gather us together, even from the grave, and crown us with *his* radiant immortality, and it will have nothing to do with our superiority but only with the glory of his grace.

God has structured into reality a forward tilt. He has built in our advantage and scheduled the happy inevitability of our debut as the children of God, fully clothed in the glory of the risen Jesus. Not that it *looks* or *feels* like that right now. The futility of this present world is formidable. You try to build something with your life but it's like a sandcastle on the beach: the waves of time wash over it and, soon, no one can tell anything was even there. But this futility isn't a flaw in God's design. That's why Paul says in verse 20, 'not by its own choice'. Reality was built against futility; futility is not intrinsic or permanent. Two thousand years ago, a second Adam entered in. We blamed him for our misery; he took it to his cross and it weighed him down into death. Then he rose up from it all with a new power of life that won't stop until the whole universe is renewed. Soon, God will uncork the cosmic champagne bottle and the whole universe will burst into explosive joy for ever. And we'll be there then, just as surely as we are here now.

Perhaps our longing for the future God has planned for us is weak because our expectations are low? Romans 8:19–23 expands our horizons exponentially. The return of Christ will not simply signal an end to suffering and futility; the whole universe will be renewed. God will dwell with redeemed humanity in the new heaven and the new earth, and we will reign with him in glorious immortality. Let's join creation, full of expectation – standing on tiptoe and craning our necks – as we pray and live in anticipation of that glorious day.

Day 8

Read Romans 8:15–30
Key verses: Romans 8:22–23

....

²²We know that the whole creation has been groaning as in the pains of childbirth right up to the present time. ²³Not only so, but we ourselves, who have the firstfruits of the Spirit, groan inwardly as we wait eagerly for our adoption to sonship, the redemption of our bodies.

Can you feel creation groaning?

It isn't just a problem here or there; a million things are broken everywhere, with endless distress, continuous sighs and unrelieved yearnings. But in this massive ordeal, God is bringing new life – creation is in 'the pains of childbirth'. God is promising us that nature 'red in tooth and claw' is only a chapter and not the conclusion. The story ends in a new world, ruled by a new human race, with God in our midst: '"He will wipe every tear from their eyes. There will be no more death" or mourning or crying or pain, for the old order of things has passed away' (Revelation 21:4).

We groan too, don't we? If you belong to Jesus, he has given you the firstfruits of the Spirit, with foretastes of your eternal glory. God has resurrected your heart from the dead so that you feel longings you never thought were real. Now you have new life within, a first instalment on your final inheritance. A person being prepared for the new universe feels not fewer but more groanings.

C. S. Lewis called it an 'inconsolable longing' (C. S. Lewis, *Surprised by Joy*, Collins, 2016, p. 82). This ache can pierce your heart at any moment. It's when you feel a yearning to be complete and finally with Christ. It can happen while in church, listening to music, holding your newborn baby or saying goodbye to a friend. The Spirit awakens this groaning with an 'Oh!' in our hearts. It's eternal life welling up within us.

And it's wonderful to think that our eternal life in the new heaven and new earth will not be ethereal, cloudy and vague. Our adoption as God's children will include 'the redemption of our bodies' (verse 23). Our whole being will finally become what God had in mind from the start. This is why Jesus died *and rose again*. The philosophers of Paul's time had a low view of the body; Paul put the resurrection of our bodies at the pinnacle of his gospel. He called it our hope (verses 24–25), the very thing we wait for with patience, because it is so worthy and glorious.

Soon our 'inconsolable longing' will be completely and utterly satisfied. Until then, our groanings serve as reminders that our hope is not in this world, although good things hint at it. Today, set your heart on God's gospel promises and wait patiently. In a little while, we will be saying with joy: 'I have come home at last! This is my real country! I belong here. This is the land I have been looking for all my life, though I never knew it till now' (C. S. Lewis, *The Last Battle*, HarperCollins, 2009, p. 210).

Day 9

Read Romans 8:15–30
Key verses: Romans 8:24–25

....

24For in this hope we were saved. But hope that is seen is no hope at all. Who hopes for what they already have? 25But if we hope for what we do not yet have, we wait for it patiently.

How would you feel if God were to give you a huge salary, a big estate and vigorous health but not himself, and the instant you died, it would be over for ever? If you were happy to settle for that, your desires would be what Pascal, the French mathematician and Catholic theologian, called 'licking the earth' (Blaise Pascal, *Penseés*, no. 666). Alternatively, your heart might say, 'This world is a nice place. God made it and will redeem it. But I'd rather have Jesus and be his than all the money in the bank. I don't mind waiting for a happiness so big that this world can't contain it.' If that's how you feel, then there is only one way to account for it: the Holy Spirit lives in you, never to leave.

And with his presence in our hearts, we wait for this glorious day 'patiently' (verse 25). Now, we don't like patience, yet this is how the early church prevailed against all the persecution and suffering. Yes, there were miracles. But look at how Paul describes his friends in Romans 16: 'they risked their lives', 'worked hard', '[fellow Jews who have been] in prison with me'. They were powerless, but they prevailed. How? By patience. They just wouldn't quit. The early theologians called patience 'the greatest virtue', 'the highest of all virtues', the secret ingredient that was 'peculiarly Christian'. They believed God was in no hurry, so they were in no hurry. They believed God was in control, so they felt no need to be in control. They believed God was powerful, so they did not become pushy and forceful. They were resilient and resourceful in the quietness of patient endurance.

Bishop Cyprian, writing to his suffering people in the third century, told them, 'As servants and worshippers of God, let us show the patience that we learn from the heavenly teachings. For that virtue we have in common with God' (Cyprian, quoted in Alan Kreider, *The Patient Ferment of the Early Church*, Baker, 2016, p. 14).

Do we want to show our modern world what God is really like? Of course. The world is facing final judgment. But God exists. He sent Jesus, who died and rose again. All the promises of God are true. And now, in this generation, it's our turn to bear witness. How? Keep going! We will prevail by hopeful patience.

In the Old Testament, Job was a righteous man whom God allowed Satan to test. In his suffering, Job asked:

> What strength do I have, that I should still hope?
>   What prospects, that I should be patient?
> (Job 6:11)

This side of the cross, we reply confidently that we are waiting for God's glory to be fully and finally revealed, and to spend eternity with him. So, with patient endurance, resilience and resourcefulness, we witness to those who are 'licking the earth' that there is something far better to live for.

Day 10

Read Romans 8:15–30
Key verse: Romans 8:28

••

29 And we know that in all things God works for the good of those who love him, who have been called according to his purpose.

This is one bold, industrial-strength promise!

Imagine a continuum. At one end is 'All things work together for good'; at the other end is 'Nothing is good'. Most of us probably find ourselves somewhere in the middle of that continuum, saying, 'I hope things work out OK.'

But, if we believe in God *at all*, we can't hold this middle position. What kind of God would promise us that some things work together for good and expect us to build a courageous life on that foundation? If there is any hope for us, it is an extreme hope that covers the worst that life throws at us. *Either* nothing is good, we suffer for nothing and have no future, *or* all things work together for good, everything about us matters and our sufferings are accelerating us into a glorious future.

How can we 'know' for sure that this gospel promise is true? Jesus. We crucified him, we chose evil, but God was working our malice for our good. He was bending our evil round to advance his good. And the resurrection of Jesus is now our wonderful destiny. When the apostle Peter preached about Jesus only months after his death, he said:

> But God knew what would happen, and his prearranged plan was carried out when Jesus was betrayed . . . You nailed him to a cross and killed him. But God released him from the horrors of death and raised him back to life.
> (Acts 2:23–24, NLT)

God does not have good days now and then so that some things work together for good; he has a good day every day so that all things work together for good. God proved that in Jesus. God has wrapped his arms widely around all things, including all evil, all your suffering, all your sins, all your tears, everything that's against you, and God is holding you. Maybe the most wonderful word in this verse is the little word 'for': '*for* those who love [God] . . . *for* [those] who [are] called according to his purpose'. You don't have to do this for yourself. You don't have to orchestrate the happy ending you long for. If you are in Christ, the resurrection of Jesus is your future, and nothing can take it away from you because God has determined to do this *for* you.

God is *for* you. It is often hard to believe but God's arms are wrapped around you; they are wrapped around your depression, cancer, strained family relationships, hurts endured in church, disappointments, sins – all of it – and he is working it together for your good. Today, trust God with 'all [your] things' and thank him that, even on the darkest of days, we can know for sure that he is on the throne and in control.

Day 11

Read Romans 8:15–30
Key verses: Romans 8:29–30

....

29 For those God foreknew he also predestined to be conformed to the image of his Son, that he might be the firstborn among many brothers and sisters. 30 And those he predestined, he also called; those he called, he also justified; those he justified, he also glorified.

These verses are not a pep talk; they are announcing to us a hope so big that it will get us through anything in this life, because our hope lies *beyond* this life.

Romans 8:29–30 is in the Bible to help us all to become confident, cheerful, resilient, pain-tolerant men and women who display Jesus in the madness of our times. Verses 29–30 explain how we can know verse 28 is true – that all things work together for our good. What larger reality guarantees that assurance? Paul doesn't point to favourable sociological trends or the latest scientific research. Nothing observable can give us certainty from beyond this world. Verses 29–30 are about God. It is as if Paul were spreading out a huge blueprint, showing us the great purposes of God spanning from eternity past to eternity future, and all of human history as a brief parenthesis within that vast field of eternity. He helps us to see just how big God's plan for us is, so that all things work together for our good.

God 'foreknew' us, which means he chose us by setting his heart on us long before we set our hearts on him (Ephesians 1:4). God 'predestined' us – he decided how we would turn out in the end – to be with Christ, like Christ and for the glory of Christ. He 'called' us. God did not hold out until we called to him; he called to us through the gospel. And because we're sinners and God can't get involved with us without forgiving us, he 'justified' us. At the cross, Jesus took our damnation so we wouldn't have to. God brought us back into his good graces, not by submerging his holy law but by satisfying it in Jesus, our willing substitute. Jesus lived for us the worthy life we have not lived and died for us the atoning death we cannot die. All we can do now is receive him with empty hands of faith. This justification does not make us morally unserious people. It makes us love the Lord and fiercely fight temptation.

In eternity future, God will perfect our personalities with the likeness of Jesus; he will raise our bodies invincible like that of the risen Jesus. Paul is so confident, he even puts it in the past tense: 'glorified', not 'will glorify'. God's plan is so unbreakable that the future is as settled as the past. No wonder all things work together for our good.

What amazing hope we have! God's plan is unbreakable; our future glory is certain. We will be with Christ, like Christ, for ever, and all things are helping us to get there. Today, praise God for all that he has done in the past, is doing for us now and will do in the future. Rejoice and rest in the glorious truth that his purpose is the power driving the universe, now and for eternity.

2 Corinthians

The apostle Paul had a close association with the church he founded in Corinth. He wrote to them four times (two of those letters are lost, with only 1 and 2 Corinthians being preserved in Scripture), and he visited them at least three times. It wasn't always an easy relationship; Paul describes his second visit as 'painful' (2 Corinthians 2:1) because he had to deal with a disciplinary issue. He delayed his next visit, not wanting to cause the congregation further grief, and instead wrote to them about his continuing concerns (in one of the lost letters). Paul wrote 2 Corinthians to pave the way for his third visit, explaining his delay and expressing his delight that the matter had been resolved (chapter 7). He encourages the believers to resume the collection for the Jerusalem church so that it would be complete when he arrived (chapters 8 – 9). Finally, in the last three chapters, he addresses the issue of his authenticity as an apostle and the 'different gospel' (11:4) false apostles are peddling. Including more auto-biographical material than any of his other letters, Paul teaches those who trust in Christ how to think about suffering, death and eternity.

Day 12

Read 2 Corinthians 4:16 – 5:10
Key verses: 2 Corinthians 4:16–17

• •

16 Therefore we do not lose heart. Though outwardly we are wasting away, yet inwardly we are being renewed day by day. 17 For our light and momentary troubles are achieving for us an eternal glory that far outweighs them all.

Why should we not lose heart?

Paul's testimony – and the testimony of countless other believers – is that the worse it gets, the better we become. Christians can grow under pressure and can have resilience in the midst of trials. Paul explains that while we're wasting away, our inner nature is being renewed day by day for a very special purpose. Our momentary affliction is preparing us for an eternal weight of glory, beyond comparison. Glory is the fullness of God's quality and character; his stunning, awesome reality. It is every aspect of his being. The Hebrew word for glory is 'weight' or 'heavy': the substance of God. Paul is saying that this trajectory of inner growth is getting us ready to receive the glory of God to ourselves. Inwardly, we are becoming increasingly like him all the time. One day 'we shall be like him, for we shall see him as he is' (1 John 3:2). In that moment of transformation, we will take on all the communicable characteristics and qualities of the almighty God, and we will be like Christ. This refreshing and renewing of our inner selves, day by day, to be ready for that moment when we become completely like Christ is the goal of every believer.

How do we get on this trajectory of inner growth? Through reading and being challenged by God's Word, the 'reproofs' of life, the counsel of friends and, especially, through affliction. James 1 tells us that God uses suffering as a friend because it works to perfect us, to form us and to give us character. I find that when trials and tribulations come, I suddenly become very God-focused. My values change. I become introspective – I look at my heart and ask, 'Lord, is there something in my life that brought this on? Is there a mistake I made in a relationship? How much of this is my fault?' I plead for God's grace; I long for his nearness. That's exactly why James 1:2 tells us to count it all joy when affliction comes our way, because God is using it to make us ready for that great day when we shall see him. It's why John writes that the one who has the hope of becoming like Christ, of receiving this eternal weight of glory, purifies himself to get ready (1 John 3:3).

Don't lose heart. Instead, be on an upward trajectory to receiving the wonderful weight of glory, the likeness of Christ that we will carry in ourselves for eternity.

> Let all true Christians remember that their best things are yet to come. Let us count it no strange thing if we have sufferings in this present time. It is a season of probation. We are yet at school. We are learning patience, gentleness, and meekness, which we could hardly learn if we had our good things now. But there is an eternal holiday yet to begin . . . It will make amends for all.
>
> (J. C. Ryle, *Expository Thoughts on the Gospel of Matthew*, Aneko Press, 2020, pp. 143–144)

Day 13

Read 2 Corinthians 4:16 – 5:10
Key verses: 2 Corinthians 4:18 – 5:1

....

4:18 *So we fix our eyes not on what is seen, but on what is unseen, since what is seen is temporary, but what is unseen is eternal.* 5:1 *For we know that if the earthly tent we live in is destroyed, we have a building from God, an eternal house in heaven, not built by human hands.*

Are you focused on the future?

Paul urges us to take our eyes off what is 'seen', the transient – our suffering and material possessions – and focus on what is eternal, the 'unseen'. Jesus had the same challenge for his disciples: 'Stop being bound to your possessions and worrying about where you're going to get your next meal or next robe. Seek first the kingdom of God, and your Father will take care of you. Sell what you have. Give it to the poor. Put your treasure in heaven instead of where moths and rust corrupt. For where your treasure is, there will your heart be also' (adapted from Luke 12). The message is that instead of being bound to the things of this earth, invest your finances, time and effort in eternity.

We also need to get our eyes off this present body and on to the future body. Can you think of anything more fragile, more vulnerable to the elements than a tent? Like a tent, our bodies are pretty fragile, but we each look forward to an eternal, resurrected body, not made with human hands. At the moment we 'groan' because of our sinful nature (2 Corinthians 5:2, 4). We each still struggle with sin and groan under its burden, longing for that heavenly body, liberated from frailty and failings.

On that day, we will no longer be ashamed because we will not be 'unclothed' (verse 4). Paul is probably referring to Adam and Eve, who saw their nakedness and were ashamed. If Jesus were to return now, like Isaiah and John, we would fall on our faces in shame before him because we are sinners still under the groaning weight of our sin. But when we finally receive those eternal, resurrected bodies, we will be clothed. Our robes will be washed white in the blood of the Lamb (Revelation 7:14). We will not be found naked before him. We will live in unhindered fellowship with him. He will be the joy of our lives.

As you feel this groaning, remember the day is coming when 'what is mortal may be swallowed up by life' (2 Corinthians 5:4).

I think of all the times when I've said to my wife, 'Ah, this is the life!' No, it's not. That day when I go home, that's when my mortality will be swallowed up in life.

Have you ever said, 'Ah, this is the life!' on these occasions?

- When you were enjoying a holiday in the sun.
- When you were relishing a good meal with friends.
- When you were appreciating your retirement.

If so, your hope is too small! Savour these and every other moment of pleasure God gives you today. But recognize that each one is a taster, whetting your appetite for the far greater eternal pleasure you will one day enjoy – being with God for ever.

Day 14

Read 2 Corinthians 4:16 – 5:10
Key verses: 2 Corinthians 5:5–8

· ·

⁵*Now the one who has fashioned us for this very purpose is God, who has given us the Spirit as a deposit, guaranteeing what is to come.*

⁶*Therefore we are always confident and know that as long as we are at home in the body we are away from the Lord.* ⁷*For we live by faith, not by sight.* ⁸*We are confident, I say, and would prefer to be away from the body and at home with the Lord.*

How can we be so sure that all God has promised will really happen?

This isn't just smoke-and-mirrors religious stuff. Look at Genesis 1: we were made in the image of God, to be image bearers, to share his glory. He prepared us for this; it's why he built us; we're wired for it. In Genesis 3, the fall left all of us, even the very best of us, severely damaged. We don't think, act, live or respond rightly. I learned a long time ago that my first instincts are almost always wrong. If you offend me, my first instinct is not to think, 'How can I forgive you and love you?' My instincts are always fallen, always broken. But Jesus came to suffer on the cross, to reclaim this damaged material of me. I wasn't for the rubbish heap; he still wanted me.

Romans 8:29 tells us, 'Those God foreknew he also predestined to be conformed to the image of his Son.' God has prepared you for this eternal weight of glory. Paul reminds us, 'He who began a good work in you will carry it on to completion until the day of Christ Jesus' (Philippians 1:6). And we can be sure about this because he's sealed us with the Holy Spirit (Ephesians 4:30).

How do you know you're going to heaven? You've been sealed. It's a done deal. The contract has been signed. The presence of the Holy Spirit in you has sealed you for the day of redemption. There's no turning back. It's guaranteed.

This knowledge breeds confidence, so Paul declares, 'We are always confident' (verse 6). It's almost as if he were saying, 'Put me on a trajectory that makes me more like Christ as I move towards that eternal weight of glory. Suffering? Bring it on! Death, you want to destroy me? You want to kill me? Hey! I'm just going home. It will accelerate the process. I'd rather be at home with the Lord. Bring it on!' Like Paul, when we grab hold of these truths by faith, we grow in confident courage.

Every time you read your Bible, pray, serve others, sacrifice for God's kingdom, submit to God's agenda and share the gospel – however weakly – these other-worldly impulses are evidence that God is transforming you. God always finishes what he starts; so these flickers of Holy Spirit life are guarantees that one day you will be like Christ. Until then, be confident that God is at work in you and join him in it – more and more relying on his Word, surrendering to his will and living for his glory.

Day 15

Read 2 Corinthians 4:16 – 5:10
Key verses: 2 Corinthians 5:9–10

....

⁹So we make it our goal to please him, whether we are at home in the body or away from it. ¹⁰For we must all appear before the judgment seat of Christ, so that each of us may receive what is due to us for the things done while in the body, whether good or bad.

Why do we live to please God?

Because we're all going to stand before the *bema* seat of Christ. In Corinth, there was a seat on which the governor sat and pronounced judgment as he heard different court cases. Paul himself had come before the *bema* seat for judgment, and he pictures Christ there. We will all be judged for what we have done, whether it be good or evil. If this were the only verse, you might imagine an old set of scales, hoping that the good would outweigh the bad so that you'd make it into heaven. But we also have the rest of Paul's writings, and the rest of the Bible, which teach us we're not saved by our works, and that appearing before Christ's judgment seat is a moment of accountability.

In 1 Corinthians 3:12–13, we are told that, when we stand before Christ, the works that we have done in the flesh will be shown to be either gold, silver and precious stones or wood, hay and stubble. The fire will prove the point. I think the fire might be the glorious presence of Jesus himself. All the things that we've done in our bodies – all those poor choices – will be the wood, hay and stubble, which will be burned away. What lasts will be only those things we've done to please God – the gold, silver and precious stones. Francis Schaeffer, the American theologian and pastor, wrote a book called *Ash Heap Lives* (Norfolk Press, 1975). I'm afraid that there are going to be a lot of 'ash heap' Christians, standing knee-deep in the ashes of their wood, hay and stubble.

Revelation 4 says that the elders worship Christ by casting their crowns at his feet, and 1 Corinthians 3 says that we'll receive rewards for the good things we've done to please God. I wonder whether, when we see Jesus, with the crowns and the rewards in our hands, we will throw them at his feet in a supreme act of worship to the worthy Christ whom we love so much. If that were to be the case, I wouldn't want to be without crowns or rewards. I wouldn't want to bring a bucket of ashes. I would want to have something. So I live to please him.

None of us wants to be an 'ash heap' Christian. We don't want to be empty-handed as we stand before God. But to be rich in rewards *then* demands a change of lifestyle and attitude *now*. People say, 'You can't take it with you,' referring to the uselessness of earthly treasures in the next life. But that's not true. A Christian does take the treasures from this world into the next. How we spend our lives now determines whether we will take wood, hay and stubble or gold, silver and precious stones into eternity. Today, in your conversations, decisions, actions and thoughts, will you truly make it your goal to please God?

1 Thessalonians

The first epistle to the Thessalonians is essentially a follow-up letter to new Christians. Persecution had forced Paul and his companions to flee the busy seaport city of Thessalonica sooner than Paul would have wished, leaving behind a group of very new Jewish and Gentile converts (Acts 17:1–10). Paul wrote to these believers from Corinth to encourage them to stand firm in the face of opposition and live godly lives. The letter also delivers instruction about the second coming of Christ – each chapter ends with a reference to this – and chapter 4 provides in-depth teaching, giving us comfort and assurance concerning the future of believers who die before Christ returns.

Day 16

Read 1 Thessalonians 4:13–18
Key verses: 1 Thessalonians 4:13–14

....

13 Brothers and sisters, we do not want you to be uninformed about those who sleep in death, so that you do not grieve like the rest of mankind, who have no hope. 14 For we believe that Jesus died and rose again, and so we believe that God will bring with Jesus those who have fallen asleep in him.

What will happen to Christians who have died before the second coming of Christ?

This is the question the Thessalonians were asking. Paul is keen to reassure these sorrowing believers that their loved ones would not miss out on Christ's coming. Indeed, they would return with him and, together with us (verses 14 and 16), receive resurrection bodies.

The return of Christ is a central part of Paul's gospel message: 'You turned to God from idols to serve the living and true God, and to wait for his Son from heaven . . . Jesus, who rescues us from the coming wrath' (1 Thessalonians 1:9–10). Clearly, these new believers must have been taught by Paul to cultivate a real spirit of immediacy in their expectation of Christ's return. Otherwise, why would they be anxious when they saw Christians in the church dying?

Paul himself certainly has this expectation. That's why he says in 1 Thessalonians 4:15, 'According to the Lord's word, we tell you that *we* who are still alive, who are left until the coming of the Lord, will certainly not precede those who have fallen asleep' (emphasis added). He doesn't say 'they', but 'we'. Is he dating the second coming? Not at all. He goes on to tell the Thessalonians, 'About times and dates we do not need to write to you, for you know very well that the day of the Lord will come like a thief in the night' (1 Thessalonians 5:1–2). Paul subscribes to the teaching of Jesus that nobody knows the day of his coming: 'But about that day or hour no one knows, not even the angels in heaven, nor the Son, but only the Father' (Matthew 24:36). Not even the Lord Jesus, as the Son of God, knows the day of his coming.

Paul, therefore, is not claiming to know the date of Jesus' second coming. It is not as if he taught that the Lord was coming soon, and events then proved him wrong.

Rather, he wants these Thessalonian believers to live in a moment-by-moment expectation of an undatable event. This is how every Christian should view the coming again of Christ, and this is the spirit of expectation we should cultivate every day. We do not know when he is coming – but we are to long for it, to live in the good of it and expect it.

No believer – alive or dead – will miss out on the glories of the second coming. We will all share in the triumph of the Lord's return. Death is not the final event; rather, we live in the certain hope of Christ's imminent return. Today, in your grief or your ordinary everyday struggles, let your meditation on this great day bring encouragement and joy to your soul.

Day 17

Read 1 Thessalonians 4:13–18
Key verses: 1 Thessalonians 4:13–14

....

> [13] *Brothers and sisters, we do not want you to be uninformed about those who sleep in death, so that you do not grieve like the rest of mankind, who have no hope.* [14] *For we believe that Jesus died and rose again, and so we believe that God will bring with Jesus those who have fallen asleep in him.*

Death is one of the few certainties of life.

Paul, full of pastoral concern, wanted the Thessalonians to be well informed. As we saw yesterday, they were anxious that fellow believers who had died would miss the second coming. So Paul allayed their fears and reminded them, and us, that we can face the sorrows of life and look forward to Jesus' return because we know that death, grief and hope have been transformed.

- *Death has been transformed*. For us believers, death is the impenetrable and irreversible reality, but for Jesus, it is the sleep from which he will shake us awake. Just as he did with Jairus' daughter in Mark 5.

- *Grief has been transformed*. How is our grief different from that of those who don't know Christ? Surprisingly perhaps, our grief is sharper. We feel grief more keenly because our emotions have been sharpened by the regenerating work of the Holy Spirit. Our grief is also different because it is in the context of eternal hope; while we grieve, we also have the glorious expectation of a joyful reunion.

- *Hope has been transformed*. The Christian hope is sure and certain because it is based on Jesus' finished work. When he died and rose again, we were associated with that death and resurrection so that we both died and rose with him. Therefore, after our death, we have the sure hope that resurrection and transformation will follow.

As Christians, we are not immune to sorrow. We face the death of loved ones just as our non-Christian neighbours do. And like Jesus weeping at Lazarus' tomb, we feel that grief keenly. But Jesus' death and resurrection mean that, for believers, death and mourning are transformed. We grieve only for a short time, knowing that one day those who are asleep in Christ will return with him and, together with them, we shall receive our resurrection bodies. If you are mourning today or facing your own mortality, allow these truths to penetrate your grief. Lift your eyes and wait expectantly for the imminent return of Christ – our sure and certain hope.

> If death tells us we're not too important to die, the gospel tells us we're so important that Christ died for us. And not because death's message about us is wrong. It isn't. On our own, we are dispensable. But joined to Christ, through our union with him, we are righteous, we are children of God, and God will not let us die any more than he left Jesus in the grave.
> (Matthew McCullough, *Remember Death*, Crossway, 2018, p. 24)

Day 18

Read 1 Thessalonians 4:13–18
Key verse: 1 Thessalonians 4:16

....

16 For the Lord himself will come down from heaven, with a loud command, with the voice of the archangel and with the trumpet call of God, and the dead in Christ will rise first.

Have you ever wondered what the return of Christ will be like?

We do not know many details, but one is guaranteed: his second coming will be very different from his first. Christ's return will be heralded with a loud command, presumably from God the Father, for who else knows when Christ is going to return and who else has the authority to give this command? God spoke when his Son was baptized (Matthew 3:17); he spoke when his Son stood on the Mount of Transfiguration (Matthew 17:5); he spoke in anticipation of Calvary: 'I have glorified [my name], and will glorify it again' (John 12:28); and, finally, he will speak the ponderous words of command: 'My beloved Son, go back again.'

The archangel Michael (see Jude 9; Daniel 10:13, 21; 12:1; Revelation 12:7), the leader of the angel armies, will announce Christ's victory. What will he say? I think he will cry out, 'The victory is won, the kingdoms of this world have become the kingdoms of our God and of his Christ and he will reign for ever and ever' (see Revelation 11:15).

And then the trumpet will sound. Why will there be a trumpet?

- It is the trumpet of Exodus 19:16 that indicates 'God is here'.

- It is the trumpet of Joel 2:1 that signals the great and awesome day of the Lord has at last come.

- It is the trumpet of Jubilee in Leviticus 25:9 that announces the release of slaves and the remission of debts.

- It is the trumpet of Isaiah 27:12–13 that sounds so the people of God scattered in Egypt and Assyria may be brought home to Zion.

- It is the trumpet of Matthew 24:31 that galvanizes the angels of God to gather God's people – past, present and future – from the four corners of the earth.

Are you looking forward to that day?

We can become so easily caught up in the good things – family, friendships, celebrations, work and holidays – that Jesus' return is not a top priority. We talk about it but don't yearn for it. We pray for it but don't tell people about it. We believe it but don't let it shape our behaviour. Today, intentionally dwell not just on the present realities of life but also on the future certainties.

Imagine the scene: Jesus returning to earth in a blaze of glory; the skies shuddering as God the Father gives the command and the archangel announces his victory. The trumpet blasts, gathering all the family of God. The glory and majesty of Christ is unmistakable. Fix this vision in your mind, let it ignite a passion in your heart for loving Christ and living for him more and more.

Day 19

Read 1 Thessalonians 4:13–18
Key verses: 1 Thessalonians 4:16–18

....

16 For the Lord himself will come down from heaven, with a loud command, with the voice of the archangel and with the trumpet call of God, and the dead in Christ will rise first. 17 After that, we who are still alive and are left will be caught up together with them in the clouds to meet the Lord in the air. And so we will be with the Lord for ever. 18 Therefore encourage one another with these words.

What will happen to us at Jesus' second coming?

Paul explains that the bodies of Christians who have died will be raised to meet their souls, which once left them, and there will be a mighty reconstitution of those who are fully redeemed. But what about those who haven't yet died? Paul says, 'We who are still alive and are left will be caught up together with them in the clouds to meet the Lord in the air.'

There is obviously symbolism here. In the Bible, the clouds represent the presence of God. After the exodus, God lived among the people in a cloudy, fiery pillar. The cloud indicated that 'God is here'. When Jesus, Peter, James and John stood on the Mount of Transfiguration, a cloud overshadowed them, and out of the cloud came the voice that said, 'This is my Son.' The message which rang out loudly and clearly was: 'God is here.' And believers will be caught up in the clouds, into the very presence of God. The air is the dominion usurped by Satan, the prince of the power of the air (Ephesians 2:2). But we will enter into his usurped dominion because he will have gone for ever. Only Jesus reigns.

The symbolism is important: with Jesus, we will be caught into the presence of God; we will enter into his eternal triumph. But there is also objectivity and reality: we will be caught up. The phrase is literally 'we will be snatched'. We will be snatched from the earth. And if we are alive on that day, we will be lifted bodily to stand before Jesus, in the fullness of redemption, as he reconciles all creation to himself.

Paul wrote these verses not to satisfy our curiosity or to give us a timeline for future events but to encourage us. We can press on through suffering and grief because

we know that, one day, we will meet the Lord and then be with him for ever.

Just as the Holy of Holies contained the dazzling presence of God in ancient Israel, so will the New Jerusalem contain his presence. The new earth's greatest miracle will be our continual, unimpeded access to the God of everlasting splendor and perpetual delight . . . God's greatest gift to us is now, and always will be, nothing less than himself.

(Randy Alcorn, 'Heaven Would Be Hell without God', 24 April 2018, <www.desiringgod.org/articles/heaven-would-be-hell-without-god>, accessed 20 September 2021)

Therefore encourage one another with these words.

(1 Thessalonians 4:18)

1 Peter

The believers scattered throughout Asia Minor (modern-day Turkey) were not prepared for the persecution they were facing. The purpose of Peter's letter was to give them confidence in God's grace despite their circumstances: 'I have written to you briefly, encouraging you and testifying that this is the true grace of God. Stand fast in it' (1 Peter 5:12). Peter encouraged these pilgrims to endure by reminding them of God's eternal purposes, the example of Jesus' suffering, the privilege of belonging to God's people, the hope they possessed and the glory awaiting them.

Day 20

Read 1 Peter 1:1–12
Key verse: 1 Peter 1:3

• •

³Praise be to the God and Father of our Lord Jesus Christ! In his great mercy he has given us new birth into a living hope through the resurrection of Jesus Christ from the dead.

How has your hope in Jesus, and the future he has promised, changed your life?

For Peter, this living hope, grounded securely in Jesus' resurrection, proved life-transforming. From Caesarea Philippi on, Jesus had spoken of his death and resurrection. But like the other disciples, Peter didn't have a category for a crucified Messiah. Messiahs weren't supposed to die; they were supposed to win and emerge triumphant. So when Jesus spoke of his impending death, Peter rebuked him: 'Never, Lord . . . This shall never happen to you!' (Matthew 16:22). Peter promised, 'Even if all fall away on account of you, I never will'

(Matthew 26:33), but later that same night, he denied ever knowing Jesus. After Jesus' crucifixion, however, when the reports from the women said that Jesus was alive, Peter ran with John to the tomb (John 20). Then, according to Paul in 1 Corinthians 15, Jesus, in his resurrected body, appeared privately to Peter before he met with the eleven other disciples. Hope sparked into life, followed by a restoration to service: 'Simon son of John [Peter], do you love me more than these?' (John 21:15).

Yet there were more massive dimensions to this hope. By this point, Peter had understood the implications. He knew that with the death and resurrection of Jesus came God's final provision for the forgiveness of sins. The promised messianic kingdom was dawning. Eternal life could be experienced now, even if not consummated until the end. And with Jesus' resurrection, there was, one day, every hope of our gaining resurrection bodies like Jesus' resurrection body. In fact, in due course, Jesus' return would come to be referred to as the 'blessed hope' of the church (Titus 2:13).

In some measure, we participate in all of this now by means of the new birth; so, with Peter, we joyfully declare, 'Praise be to the God and Father of our Lord Jesus Christ! In his great mercy he has given us new birth into a living hope through the resurrection of Jesus Christ from the dead.'

We have hope in this life and the next because of Jesus' resurrection. His death and resurrection are the irrefutable proof that our sins are forgiven, our relationship with God is restored and eternal life can be experienced now. We also have the promise that we will have resurrection bodies and spend for ever with God in the new heaven and new earth. Today, praise God for his 'great mercy' towards us: 'he does not treat us as our sins deserve' (Psalm 103:10). Thank God that, through Christ, we have new birth into a living hope, which transforms our lives now and for ever.

Day 21

Read 1 Peter 1:1–12
Key verses: 1 Peter 1:3–5

....

> [3] *Praise be to the God and Father of our Lord Jesus Christ! In his great mercy he has given us new birth into a living hope through the resurrection of Jesus Christ from the dead,* [4] *and into an inheritance that can never perish, spoil or fade. This inheritance is kept in heaven for you,* [5] *who through faith are shielded by God's power until the coming of the salvation that is ready to be revealed in the last time.*

Are you looking forward to your inheritance? Not from your parents or a distant relative, but the inheritance God has for you.

There is a parallel in verse 3 and verses 4 and 5 between new birth into a living hope and new birth into an inheritance that can never perish. When Peter writes of this imperishable inheritance, doubtless he is recalling Jesus' teaching about treasure in the Sermon on the Mount:

Do not store up for yourselves treasures on earth, where moths and vermin destroy, and where thieves break in and steal. But store up for yourselves treasures in heaven, where moths and vermin do not destroy, and where thieves do not break in and steal.
(Matthew 6:19–20)

Here, the focus is not on treasure quite so much as on inheritance. Peter and his readers have an Old Testament background in mind, picturing the Israelites' inheritance first and foremost to be the land – not only given to the Israelites as a whole but also parcelled out to each clan, each extended family, with lasting rights of ownership, at least on paper. The Old Testament people of God were aliens and pilgrims until they entered the Promised Land and received their inheritance.

This does not mean they were utterly destitute, for there was a sense in which, although they were not yet in the land promised to them, the land was in principle theirs. It was therefore the Promised Land; they looked forward to it with hope. In due course, God brought about the accomplishment of that hope, and they entered into their inheritance.

Peter's description of our inheritance emerges from this God-ordained Old Testament model. We, too, are aliens and pilgrims. This does not mean we are paupers waiting for an inheritance that is in no sense ours. We are enriched in the certainty of the promise, and Peter insists that some part of it has already come to us. We have a clear title to the inheritance that God has reserved for us, and we also possess a down payment.

Because of Christ's work on the cross, you qualify to receive the inheritance God has planned – your name is on the title deeds (Colossians 1:12–13). The Holy Spirit living within you is the first instalment and the promise of the full measure to come (Ephesians 1:14). Today, if you are feeling hopeless or find yourself doubting God's promise, make Paul's prayer your own: 'I pray that the eyes of your heart may be enlightened in order that you may know the hope to which he has called you, the riches of his glorious inheritance in his holy people' (Ephesians 1:18).

Day 22

Read 1 Peter 1:1–12
Key verses: 1 Peter 1:3–5

....

³ *Praise be to the God and Father of our Lord Jesus Christ! In his great mercy he has given us new birth into a living hope through the resurrection of Jesus Christ from the dead, ⁴and into an inheritance that can never perish, spoil or fade. This inheritance is kept in heaven for you, ⁵who through faith are shielded by God's power until the coming of the salvation that is ready to be revealed in the last time.*

Can we be sure of receiving our inheritance? Can we bank our lives on it?

Peter says that our inheritance can 'never perish, spoil or fade'. These words are used in various Old Testament descriptions in Greek, concerning things that happened to the land. Sometimes the people are run out of the land or marauding troops come in, but the land is still there and does not perish. According to 2 Peter 3, the whole universe will finally burn up with such a fierce heat that even the elements will be devoured, but our inheritance won't burn up; it's reserved in heaven for us.

In Ancient Israel's concept of things, the land could also be polluted by the sins of the people, but the new heaven and the new earth have no sin in them. They are never defiled; they cannot be spoiled. Peter actually calls the new heaven and the new earth 'the home of righteous-ness' (2 Peter 3:13). There will be no shred of bitterness, hatred, arrogance, greed, lust, envy, jealousy, murder or resentment – nothing to spoil or corrode our inheritance.

The land could even be parched; its fruitfulness could fade, as in the days of drought imposed by God himself under the ministry of Elijah. But our inheritance is salva-tion consummated in the new heaven and the new earth, where there will never ever be any sort of drought again.

This inheritance is kept in heaven for us, and we are kept for it. God keeps your inheritance for *you* (verse 4). At the same time, he keeps *you* for the inheritance, shielded by God's power (verse 5). Otherwise, the inheritance could be nicely parked up while we wander off in rebellion and are damned. But no, God keeps his own people by his power, preserving us as he preserves the inherit-ance for us; as we hope for it and eagerly anticipate our inheritance, we are shielded by God's power, through faith. This is God's means of keeping us (verse 5), as it is God's means of saving us. This faith and hope are both grounded in God: 'Through him you believe in God, who raised him from the dead and glorified him, and so your faith and hope are in God' (1 Peter 1:21).

Our inheritance is utterly secure. It could not be more so because God himself is our guarantee. It will be everlasting and infinitely satisfying.

> We will be less sinful in the next life than we are now [indeed, for we won't be sinful at all], but we will not be any more secure in the next life than we are now. If you are united to Christ, you are as good as in heaven already.
>
> (Dane Ortlund, *Gentle and Lowly*, Crossway, 2020, p. 195)

Revelation

As early as the end of the first century, the future of the church hung in the balance. False teaching and internal division were rife. Domitian, the Roman emperor, had instigated persecution against those who would not worship him as lord. The apostle John, exiled on the island of Patmos, wrote to encourage believers to resist the demands of the emperor. He exhorted them to beware the devil's schemes and to look forward to Christ's triumphant return, which would ensure their complete vindication.

The book of Revelation is full of amazing visions and is highly symbolic. We won't understand every detail, but God's sovereignty is in no doubt. Christ's message is to resist compromising our faith and to stand firm in trials because he will return soon to establish the new heaven and the new earth, and we will then enjoy his presence for ever.

Day 23

Read Revelation 4:1–11
Key verses: Revelation 4:1–2

....

¹After this I looked, and there before me was a door standing open in heaven. And the voice I had first heard speaking to me like a trumpet said, 'Come up here, and I will show you what must take place after this.' ²At once I was in the Spirit, and there before me was a throne in heaven with someone sitting on it.

What is God doing now?

He is on his throne in heaven.

This vision of God's throne room in chapter 4 comes naturally after chapters 2 and 3, where God is giving the church a spiritual health check. There are lots of wonderful things to commend, but also some serious problems and challenges. The church is under attack: virtually all the seven churches are facing persecution.

They are being invaded by false teachers. The most alarming thing of all is the spiritual decline within the churches, almost bordering on apostasy.

Christ looks at the church in Ephesus and says, 'Your love for me was so strong, how sad to see how weak and cold it has become.' To the church in Sardis, he says, 'You have such a fantastic reputation! Everyone's talking about how alive you are, but it's only a reputation. You are spiritually dead.' Worst of all, to the church in Laodicea, he says, 'You're so compromised, you make me sick.'

You can imagine the apostle John feeling discouraged and fearing for the future of the church. But God takes him to heaven and shows him this glorious vision. The point is that even when the church is feeble, even when the world seems to turn its back on God completely, the ultimate place of authority in the universe is his throne. The word 'throne' is a key word in Revelation. It is used about sixty times in the New Testament, forty-seven times in the book of Revelation and fourteen times in this chapter. The theme of this chapter of Revelation, and of the whole Bible, is the absolute authority of the throne of God.

God isn't looking at the universe, wringing his hands and getting frustrated. He is on his throne. God has plans for his cosmos, his church and you. Perhaps you have trials and troubles. You need to take this to heart: God is still on the throne – you are in God's hands; your children are in God's hands; and your church is in God's hands. There is a God in heaven who reigns, and he loves you. The sovereignty of God is the softest pillow on which Christians can lay their heads.

Are you fearful about the future for your children, for Christian believers or for the nation's spiritual health? God is on the throne. Meditate on this truth as you pray about world events, your family relationships, circumstances and sadness. Rest and rely on God's gracious sovereignty, trusting that he is working for your good and for his glory.

You, LORD, reign for ever;
    your throne endures from generation to generation.
(Lamentations 5:19)

Day 24

Read Revelation 4:1–11
Key verses: Revelation 4:3, 5

· ·

> [3] *And the one who sat there had the appearance of jasper and ruby. A rainbow that shone like an emerald encircled the throne . . .* [5] *From the throne came flashes of lightning, rumblings and peals of thunder.*

Have you ever been awestruck? Have you been left speechless, gazing at a breathtaking sunset or holding a newborn baby?

John is awestruck in heaven's throne room. When he describes Christ's majesty in Revelation 1, he says that Jesus is like 'a son of man'. When Jesus went back to heaven, he didn't leave his humanity behind; he still has it. But when John describes God the Father sitting on the throne, he can't use those kinds of pictures. Finite human language struggles to put God's majesty into words. He has the '*appearance* of jasper' and is encircled by a rainbow that shines '*like* an emerald'.

Surrounding the throne are twenty-four other thrones, and sitting upon them are twenty-four elders. These elders represent the totality of the redeemed community. They are dressed in white, with crowns of gold on their heads: redeemed by Christ's blood, they reign with Christ, his victor's crown upon each of their heads. Isn't it encouraging that those closest to heaven's throne are the redeemed community? The church, the people of God, are closest to God's heart. When we become disillusioned with the church and are tempted to criticize it, we need to remember, it is God's church.

John describes the 'flashes of lightning, rumblings and peals of thunder' coming from the throne (verse 5). The Greek uses the present tense: this is continually happening. Just as, at Sinai, the ground shook and the air was filled with light, this is a picture of the holiness of God. Before the throne, the seven spirits of God are blazing. There aren't seven spirits. Rather, seven is a picture of the fullness of the Holy Spirit. Here, we see the grand mystery of the Trinity: the Father on the throne; in front of the throne, the Spirit of God; and, in chapter 5, the Lamb who was slain.

Then, around the throne are four living creatures. They have faces like the cherubim in Ezekiel 1 and six wings like the seraphim in Isaiah 6. They represent the animate creation God has made. The lion represents the wild beasts; the ox, domestic beasts; the eagle, flying beasts; and man, the pinnacle of creation. This is a picture of the whole of creation joining the redeemed community in heaven to worship God.

What's the overall impression of this vision? The flashes of lightning, the sounds of thunder, the movement of angels . . . It is a picture of awe, mystery, majesty and wonder. Are you looking forward to spending eternity with God? It is going to be glorious!

The reality of the throne room of heaven is so awesome because God is glorious, majestic, magnificent and mysterious. We too easily settle for a pygmy god who is made in our image: one who is a friend but not fierce, and familiar but not flawless. Today, gaze on John's vision; recapture your awe and reverent fear of God. Don't settle for a God who is too small.

> Who among the gods
>   is like you, Lord?
> Who is like you –
>   majestic in holiness,
> awesome in glory,
>   working wonders?
> (Exodus 15:11)

Day 25

Read Revelation 4:1–11
Key verses: Revelation 4:8, 10–11

....

⁸*Day and night [the living creatures] never stop saying:*

> *'"Holy, holy, holy*
> *is the Lord God Almighty,"*
> *who was, and is, and is to come.'*

¹⁰*The twenty-four elders . . . lay their crowns before the throne and say:*

> ¹¹*'You are worthy, our Lord and God,*
> *to receive glory and honour and power,*
> *for you created all things,*
> *and by your will they were created*
> *and have their being.'*

What style of music is appropriate? What instruments should we use?

In many churches, worship is a hotly contested subject. In heaven, it is not debated, only demonstrated.

Every picture of heaven given in Revelation always speaks about the worship and adoration of the One who's on the throne and the Lamb. The creatures' worship is continual: 'day and night they never stop saying: " 'Holy, holy, holy is the Lord God Almighty' " ' (verse 8). The elders join this God-centred adoration. They are not concerned about themselves or their feelings; their attention is on God and on his majesty and wonder. These twenty-four elders (representing the redeemed) and creation (represented by the four living creatures) lift up their hearts in praise and worship.

The focus of this worship begins with who God is (verse 8). The simple, profound, fundamental truth about God is his holiness. It is the sheer *Godness* of God that marks him out as God: his awesome majesty, his absolute purity, his holiness. He is the Holy One, the Almighty One, the Eternal and Unchanging God, who was, and who is, and who is to come. We are creatures of a moment; like John, dust and ashes standing before the eternal One.

As the elders lay their crowns before him, the focus of their worship shifts from who God is to what he has done (verse 11). God created everything out of nothing, by the power of his word and for the purpose of his glory. The whole of the cosmos begins with God, belongs to God and exists because God wills it, and it will one day glorify God.

We need to recapture the wonder of God that the living creatures and elders proclaim so that we, too, respond with such praise. We were created, redeemed and destined for adoration. The purpose of Revelation 4 is to cause us to lift our eyes to the heavenly throne, to see the power, majesty and might of God, and cry, 'Wow! What a God!'

Worship will never be redundant. Our worship today, along with that of believers already in heaven, will continue throughout eternity because the worth of who God is and what he has done is inexhaustible. Today, worship God with holy abandon because he is forever worthy of our adoration.

> Praise, my soul, the King of heaven,
> to his feet your tribute bring;
> ransomed, healed, restored, forgiven,
> who like you his praise should sing?
> Alleluia, alleluia!
> Praise the everlasting King.
> (Henry Francis Lyte, 1834)

Day 26

Read Revelation 7:9–12
Key verse: Revelation 7:9

....

⁹After this I looked, and there before me was a great multitude that no one could count, from every nation, tribe, people and language, standing before the throne and before the Lamb. They were wearing white robes and were holding palm branches in their hands.

Would you like a glimpse of heaven?

The book of Revelation presents to us the completion of the great drama of salvation. It lifts the curtain – it is, literally, an 'unveiling' – and, in chapter 7, we are given a vision of heaven.

John gives his first-century believers a glorious vision of God's throne surrounded by representatives from every part of the globe. He piles up the expressions – 'nation', 'tribe', 'people', 'language' – to show that the redeemed,

God's family, aren't from a restricted group but from all over the world. And this international community is in-numerable: 'a great multitude that no one could count'.

Do you remember when God said to Abraham, 'I will surely bless you and make your descendants as numerous as the stars in the sky and as the sand on the seashore' (Genesis 22:17)? This is John's vision: all Abraham's true offspring, all the servants of God from down through the centuries and from every part of the world, as far as his eyes could see – a countless number streaming in from every direction – but each one standing before the throne and in front of the Lamb. If God is drawing people from every tribe, language, people and nation, then his mission is by definition worldwide. As Christians, we are part of a global family, and we need to be passionately committed to making John's international vision a reality.

Today, we find it increasingly difficult to assert that the Christian faith is for the whole world. In an age that prizes tolerance, it is not easy to proclaim the absolute truth of a universal Saviour. And further, our own horizons are shrinking. It is not uncommon for Christians to focus almost exclusively on personal, family or local church life. These are proper concerns, but the tribalism, nationalism and individualism of our culture should not be allowed to extinguish John's vision. We can't truly worship God and at the same time appear to be totally indifferent about whether or not anyone else is worshipping him.

Jesus declared, 'This gospel of the kingdom will be preached in the whole world as a testimony to all nations, and then the end will come' (Matthew 24:14). Thank God, in recent years we have seen a greater advance of the church's global mission than in any previous century. John's vision is becoming a reality, and now, more than ever, God's international purposes must be in our hearts and on our lips, touching our wallets, shaping our prayers and transforming our churches.

> God is pursuing with omnipotent passion a worldwide purpose of gathering joyful worshippers for himself from every tribe and tongue and people and nation. He has an inexhaustible enthusiasm for the supremacy of his name among the nations. Therefore, let us bring our affections into line with his, and, for the sake of his name, let us renounce the quest for worldly comforts and join his global purpose.
>
> (John Piper, *Let the Nations Be Glad*, IVP, 2010, p. 62)

Day 27

Read Revelation 7:9–12
Key verses: Revelation 7:11–12

....

[11] All the angels were standing round the throne and round the elders and the four living creatures. They fell down on their faces before the throne and worshipped God, [12] saying:

> *'Amen!*
> *Praise and glory*
> *and wisdom and thanks and honour*
> *and power and strength*
> *be to our God for ever and ever.*
> *Amen!'*

'Of this good man let this be written, heaven was in him before he was in heaven.' These words describe the Puritan preacher Richard Sibbes. The seventeenth-century writer Izaak Walton is said to have penned them in his own copy of *The Returning Backslider*, a book by Sibbes.

Are they true of you?

In the Greek, each of the seven qualities listed in verse 12 is preceded by 'the'. In each case, it is not 'a' but 'the' praise, 'the' glory, and so on, above all others that should go to our God for ever and ever. On that day, when all God's people are finally gathered in, the focus will be the glory of God. And we have cause to anticipate that celebration. Psalm 96:3 exhorts us to 'declare his glory among the nations'. We are to proclaim the greatness of God above all other gods. Our task is to call our friends, neighbours and all people to worship him. Indeed, we can say that Jesus came as an evangelist for worshippers.

> Missions is not the ultimate goal of the church. Worship is. Missions exists because worship doesn't. Worship is ultimate, not missions, because God is ultimate, not man. When this age is over, and the countless millions of the redeemed fall on their faces before the throne of God, missions will be no more. It is a temporary necessity. But worship abides forever. So worship is the fuel and goal of missions.
>
> (John Piper, *Let the Nations Be Glad*, IVP, 2010, p. 7).

Perhaps the reason for our lack of concern, our limited giving to missions and our half-hearted prayers is our little-felt emotion of burning desire for God's glory. Henry

Martyn, a nineteenth-century missionary to India said, 'I could not endure existence if Jesus was not glorified. It would be hell for me if he were thus dishonoured' (quoted in John Stott with Tim Chester, *The World: A Mission to Be Accomplished*, IVP, 2019, p. 78).

Do we have a similar passion for God's glory? That will be the focus in the new heaven and new earth – and if heaven is in our hearts now, that will be our longing, too. And if we are gripped by God's glory, we will want to further God's mission. Our prayer, and our consequent effort, will echo that of the psalmist: 'Let the peoples praise you, O God; let all the peoples praise you!' (Psalm 67:3, ESV).

When Christ returns Habakkuk's prophesy will be realized: 'The earth will be filled with the knowledge of the glory of the LORD as the waters cover the sea' (Habakkuk 2:14). How do we prepare for that day? How do we increase our desire for God's glory? As in heaven, it begins with worship, focusing on God's character and greatness, not our own. It is a prayerful, conscious, moment-by-moment obedience and willing surrender of ourselves and our lesser loves.

> For from him and through him and for him are all things.
>   To him be the glory for ever! Amen.
> (Romans 11:36)

Day 28

Read Revelation 21:1–27
Key verses: Revelation 21:1–2

....

¹Then I saw 'a new heaven and a new earth,' for the first heaven and the first earth had passed away, and there was no longer any sea. ²I saw the Holy City, the new Jerusalem, coming down out of heaven from God, prepared as a bride beautifully dressed for her husband.

What will the new heaven and new earth be like?

John describes it as 'the Holy City', not built by human hands but coming down from God (verse 2). God's city, his work, will be characterized by security, community, immensity, purity, luminosity and intimacy.

- *Security*. There are wonderfully thick walls (verses 17–18).

- *Community*. God is dwelling among his people (verse 3). The names of the twelve tribes of Israel are written on the gates, and the names of the twelve apostles are written on the foundations (verses 12–14). At the end of time, there is one great, united family of God. The barrier, the dividing wall of hostility between Jew and non-Jew, broken down in Christ (Ephesians 2:14), has produced the one people of God, sharing eternity.

- *Immensity*. It measures 12,000 stadia cubed (Revelation 21:16). That is 1,400 miles by 1,400 miles by 1,400 miles. The holy city is huge! There is room here for everyone who comes to Christ. Sharing the gospel is not a sideshow in history; it is the Master's plan. His plan of the ages is to bring countless sinners home as sons and daughters of God: 'a great multitude that no one could count' (Revelation 7:9).

- *Purity*. 'Nothing impure will ever enter' (Revelation 21:27). With great sensitivity, and tears in our eyes, we have to warn people of the judgment to come (Revelation 20:11–15). The stakes are high, for there is heaven to gain and hell to shun. That is what makes human decisions so important and gospel witness essential and urgent.

- *Luminosity*. There is no more darkness because God gives light to the heavenly city and Jesus, the Lamb of God, is its lamp (Revelation 21:23–25).

• *Intimacy*. We are heading to a new depth of intimacy with God. In the new heaven and new earth, God will dwell with his people (verse 3). There is no need for a temple where people come to worship God because he is everywhere (verse 22). The city is also described as a perfect cube (verse 16). Why? Because that is what the ancient holy of holies in Solomon's temple was (1 Kings 6:20). Now this whole city, this whole new creation, is a holy of holies, where we will *see* the Lord: 'they will see his face, and his name will be on their foreheads' (Revelation 22:4). This is what we were made for!

> I have heard of him, and though I have not
> seen his face, unceasingly I have adored him.
> But I shall SEE him!
> Yes, we shall actually gaze upon the exalted
>   Redeemer!
> Realize the thought!
> Is there not a young heaven within it?
> You shall see the hand that was nailed for you;
> you shall kiss the very lips that said, 'I thirst';
> you shall see the thorn-crowned head,
> and bow with all the blood-washed throng!
> You, the chief of sinners, shall adore him who
>   washed you

in his blood; when you shall have a vision of his glory. Faith is precious, but what must sight be?
(C. H. Spurgeon, *Spurgeon's Sermons, Volume 05*, Anthony Uyl (ed.), Devoted Publishing, 2017, p. 338)

Day 29

Read Revelation 22:1–21
Key verses: Revelation 22:1–2

....

¹Then the angel showed me the river of the water of life, as clear as crystal, flowing from the throne of God and of the Lamb ²down the middle of the great street of the city. On each side of the river stood the tree of life, bearing twelve crops of fruit, yielding its fruit every month.

Home is the place where you can raid the fruit bowl without asking.

In God's home, there is fruit to eat and refreshment after a long journey. There is a river of cool, fresh, unpolluted water, flowing out from the throne of God. God has been providing water for his people all the way through the Bible: water from the rock in Exodus 17, and Psalm 46:4 declares, 'There is a river whose streams make glad the city of God.' Jesus said, 'Let anyone who is thirsty come to me and drink' (John 7:37). All these images and events point to a truth about God's home – it has a source of never-failing refreshment, and you will never have tasted water like it.

'On each side of the river stood the tree of life' – is it one great tree, which the water flows through, or are there trees down either side of the river? It doesn't really matter. The point is that every month there is different, fresh fruit to eat, and there are no restrictions as there were in Eden.

Neither is there any curse – not on the ground, not on childbirth; no curse of the law, no death. All are completely overcome through Christ, his cross and his coming. We shall 'see his face' (Revelation 22:4): all the instincts to hide that started to arise within the human race in the Garden of Eden will be gone. He will write his name on our foreheads: his name of ownership, the expression of his character will be in us and on us. The Jewish high priest used to bear God's name on his forehead, and he alone could enter God's presence – only one man, from one tribe, on one day, once a year. But we are going to be able to have access to the Lord all the time.

And all this will never end: we 'will reign for ever and ever' (verse 5). We will never be thrown out like Adam and Eve were thrown out of Eden. This 'for ever' security is one of the deepest gifts that a bridegroom can give his bride. It doesn't always work out that way in life, sadly. The best any of us can offer a spouse is 'til death do us part', but God is never going to die. The safety and security he offers us is endless.

> Our 'forever home' is waiting. It will be a place of many longed-for gifts, such as security, peace and refreshment. But it will be 'home' simply because God is there. We will delight in his presence endlessly.

> We will constantly be more amazed with God, more in love with God, and thus ever more relishing his presence and our relationship with him. Our experience of God will never reach its consummation . . . It will deepen and develop, intensify and amplify, unfold and increase, broaden and balloon.
>
> (Sam Storms, quoted in Randy Alcorn, *Eternal Perspectives*, Tyndale, 2012, p. 240)

Day 30

Read Revelation 22:1–21
Key verses: Revelation 22:6–7

••

⁶The angel said to me, 'These words are trust-worthy and true. The Lord, the God who inspires the prophets, sent his angel to show his servants the things that must soon take place.'

⁷'Look, I am coming soon! Blessed is the one who keeps the words of the prophecy written in this scroll.'

How can we know for certain that the new heaven and new earth will be established?

It comes down to whom we trust. Powerfully, we are reminded that the One who speaks to us is the Lord himself: 'He who was seated on the throne said, "I am making everything new!" Then he said, "Write this down, for these words are trustworthy and true"' (Revelation 21:5). The same emphasis continues in chapter 22: 'These words are trustworthy and true' (verse 6). We can trust these promises about Christ's return and the new heaven and the new earth because they are God's words and 'the word of our God stands forever' (Isaiah 40:8, NKJV).

Jesus himself reminds us three times, 'I am coming soon' (Revelation 22:7, 12 and 20). So, why such a delay? 'Soon' does not mean 'immediately'; it means 'imminently', or perhaps 'surprisingly' better captures the idea. The point is that every day we are to anticipate and look forward to his coming and so live each day to his glory.

Because the Lord is returning, what kind of churches do we need? Obedient and responsive ones: 'Look, I am coming soon! Blessed is the one who keeps the words of the prophecy written in this scroll' (verse 7). We also need to walk closely with Christ, worshipping God (verses 8–9) and staying spiritually clean: 'Blessed are those who wash their robes, that they may have the right to the tree of life and may go through the gates into the city' (verse 14). We need daily and hourly to respond to the invitation: 'The Spirit and the bride say, "Come!" And let the one who hears say, "Come!" Let the one who is thirsty come; and let the one who wishes take the free gift of the water of life' (verse 17).

In short, we need to share with others this invitation of a wonderful, ultimate, eternal home.

When friends or colleagues mock the certainty of our future hope, when doubts overwhelm us or our 'momentary affliction' (2 Corinthians 4:17, ESV) seems never-ending, lean on Christ's true and trustworthy words: 'I am coming soon.' As you hold fast to this promise, keep coming to Christ – in worship and obedience, and for forgiveness and cleansing. Pray today that the cry of our hearts truly would be: 'Come, Lord Jesus' (Revelation 22:20).

For further study

If you would like to read more on the theme of hope, you might find this selection of books helpful.

- Randy Alcorn, *Heaven* (Tyndale, 2009).

- Randy Alcorn, *We Shall See God: Charles Spurgeon's Classic Devotional Thoughts on Heaven* (Tyndale, 2011).

- D. A. Carson and Jeff Robinson Sr (eds.), *Coming Home: Essays on the New Heaven and New Earth* (Crossway, 2017).

- Sharon James, *The Dawn of Heaven Breaks: Anticipating Eternity* (Evangelical Press, 2007).

- Scot McKnight, *The Heaven Promise: Engaging the Bible's Truth about Life to Come* (Hodder & Stoughton, 2015).

- Bruce Milne, *The Message of Heaven and Hell*, The Bible Speaks Today (IVP, 2002).

- Marcus Nodder, *What Happens When I Die? And Other Questions about Heaven, Hell and the Life to Come* (The Good Book Company, 2013).

- James Paul, *What on Earth Is Heaven?* (IVP, 2021).
- N. T. Wright, *Surprised by Hope* (SPCK, 2011).

Keswick Ministries

Our purpose

Keswick Ministries exists to inspire and equip Christians to love and live for Christ in his world.

God's purpose is to bring his blessing to all the nations of the world (Genesis 12:3). That promise of blessing, which touches every aspect of human life, is ultimately fulfilled through the life, death, resurrection, ascension and future return of Christ. All the people of God are called to participate in his missionary purposes, wherever he may place them. The central vision of Keswick Ministries is to see the people of God equipped, inspired and refreshed to fulfil that calling, directed and guided by God's Word in the power of his Spirit, for the glory of his Son.

Our priorities

There are three fundamental priorities which shape all that we do as we look to serve the local church.

- *Hearing God's Word*: the Scriptures are the foundation for the church's life, growth and mission, and Keswick Ministries is committed to preach and teach God's

Word in a way that is faithful to Scripture and relevant to Christians of all ages and backgrounds.

- *Becoming like God's Son*: from its earliest days, the Keswick movement has encouraged Christians to live godly lives in the power of the Spirit, to grow in Christ-likeness and to live under his Lordship in every area of life. This is God's will for his people in every culture and generation.

- *Serving God's mission*: the authentic response to God's Word is obedience to his mission, and the inevitable result of Christlikeness is sacrificial service. Keswick Ministries seeks to encourage committed discipleship in family life, work and society, and energetic engagement in the cause of world mission.

Our ministry

- *Keswick Convention*. The Convention attracts some 12,000 to 15,000 Christians from the UK and around the world to Keswick every summer. It provides Bible teaching for all ages, vibrant worship, a sense of unity across generations and denominations, and an inspirational call to serve Christ in the world. It caters for children of all ages and has a strong youth and young adult programme. And it all takes place in the beautiful

Lake District – a perfect setting for rest, recreation and refreshment.

- *Keswick fellowship*. For more than 140 years, the work of Keswick has affected churches worldwide, not just through individuals being changed but also through Bible conventions that originate or draw their inspiration from the Keswick Convention. Today, there is a network of events that share Keswick Ministries' priorities across the UK and in many parts of Europe, Asia, North America, Australia, Africa and the Caribbean. Keswick Ministries is committed to strengthening the network in the UK and beyond through prayer, news and co-operative activity.

- *Keswick teaching and training*. Keswick Ministries is developing a range of inspiring, Bible-centred teaching and training that focuses on equipping believers for 'whole-of-life' discipleship. This builds on the same concern that started the Convention, that all Christians live godly lives in the power of the Spirit in all spheres of life in God's world. Some of the smaller and more intensive events focus on equipping attendees, while others focus on inspiring them. Some are for pastors, others for those in different forms of church leadership, while many are for any Christian. The aim of all the courses is for the participants to return home refreshed to serve.

- *Keswick resources.* Keswick Ministries produces a range of books, devotionals, study guides and digital resources to inspire and equip the church to live for Christ. The printed resources focus on the core foundations of Christian life and mission, and help the people of God in their walk with Christ. The digital resources make teaching and sung worship from the Keswick Convention available in a variety of ways.

Our unity

The Keswick movement worldwide has adopted a key Pauline statement to describe its gospel inclusivity: 'All one in Christ Jesus' (Galatians 3:28). Keswick Ministries works with evangelicals from a wide variety of church backgrounds, on the understanding that they share a commitment to the essential truths of the Christian faith as set out in our statement of belief.

Our contact details

T: 017687 80075
E: info@keswickministries.org
W: www.keswickministries.org
Mail: Keswick Ministries, Rawnsley Centre, Main Street, Keswick, Cumbria CA12 5NP, England

Food for the Journey THEMES

The Food for the Journey: Themes offers daily devotions from well-loved Bible teachers at the Keswick Convention, exploring how particular themes are woven through the Bible and what we can learn from them today. In a convenient, pocket-sized format, these books are ideal to accompany you wherever you go.

978 1 78974 163 6

'A rich feast! . . . We can still have joy in Jesus, even when there are tears in our eyes.'
Edrie Mallard

978 1 78974 102 5

'Full of essential theology, especially important when the going gets tough.'
Catherine Campbell

978 1 78974 169 8

'The ideal reboot for a flagging devotional life.'
Julian Hardyman

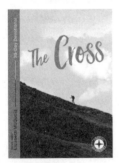

978 1 78974 191 9

'A must read.'
Gavin Calver

978 1 78974 190 2

'A beautiful collection.'
Elinor Magowan

978 1 78974 341 8

'A gripping . . . examination of God's faithfulness.'
Sharon Hastings

Available from your local Christian bookshop or **www.ivpbooks.com**

Related titles from IVP

Food for the Journey

The Food for the Journey series offers daily devotionals from well-loved Bible teachers at the Keswick Convention in an ideal pocket-sized format – to accompany you wherever you go.

Available in the series

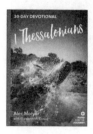

1 Thessalonians

Alec Motyer with

Elizabeth McQuoid

978 1 78359 439 9

2 Timothy

Michael Baughen with

Elizabeth McQuoid

978 1 78359 438 2

Colossians

Steve Brady with

Elizabeth McQuoid

978 1 78359 722 2

Ezekiel

Liam Goligher with

Elizabeth McQuoid

978 1 78359 603 4

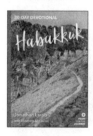

Habakkuk

Jonathan Lamb with

Elizabeth McQuoid

978 1 78359 652 2

Hebrews

Charles Price with

Elizabeth McQuoid

978 1 78359 611 9

James

Stuart Briscoe with

Elizabeth McQuoid

978 1 78359 523 5

John 14 – 17

Simon Manchester with

Elizabeth McQuoid

978 1 78359 495 5

Available from your local Christian bookshop or **www.ivpbooks.com**

Food for the Journey

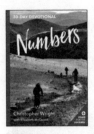   

Numbers

Christopher Wright
with Elizabeth
McQuoid
978 1 78359 720 8

Revelation 1 - 3

Paul Mallard with
Elizabeth McQuoid
978 1 78359 712 3

Romans 5 - 8

John Stott with
Elizabeth McQuoid
978 1 78359 718 5

Ruth

Alistair Begg with
Elizabeth McQuoid
978 1 78359 525 9

Praise for the series

'This devotional series is biblically rich,
theologically deep and full of wisdom . . .
I recommend it highly.' **Becky Manley Pippert,**
speaker, author of *Out of the Saltshaker and
into the World* and creator of the Live/Grow/
Know course and series of books

'These devotional guides are excellent tools.'
**John Risbridger, Minister and Team Leader,
Above Bar Church, Southampton**

'These bite-sized banquets . . . reveal our
loving Father weaving the loose and messy
ends of our everyday lives into his beautiful,
eternal purposes in Christ.' **Derek Burnside,
Principal, Capernwray Bible School**

'I would highly recommend this series of
30-day devotional books to anyone seeking
a tool that will help [him or her] to gain a
greater love of scripture, or just simply . . .
to do something out of devotion. Whatever
your motivation, these little books are a must-
read.' **Claud Jackson, *Youthwork* Magazine**

Available from your local Christian bookshop or **www.ivpbooks.com**

Related teaching CD and DVD packs

CD PACKS

1 Thessalonians
SWP2203D (5-CD pack)

2 Timothy
SWP2202D (4-CD pack)

Colossians
SWP2318D (4-CD pack)

Ezekiel
SWP2263D (5-CD pack)

Habakkuk
SWP2299D (5-CD pack)

Hebrews
SWP2281D (5-CD pack)

James
SWP2239D (4-CD pack)

John 14 – 17
SWP2238D (5-CD pack)

Numbers
SWP2317D (5-CD pack)

Revelation
SWP2300D (5-CD pack)

Romans 5 – 8
SWP2316D (4-CD pack)

Ruth
SWP2280D (5-CD pack)

Available from www.essentialchristian.com

Related teaching CD and DVD packs

DVD PACKS

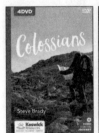

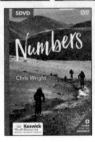

Colossians
SWP2318A (4-DVD pack)

Ezekiel
SWP2263A (5-DVD pack)

Habakkuk
SWP2299A (5-DVD pack)

John 14 – 17
SWP2238A (5-DVD pack)

Numbers
SWP2317A (5-DVD pack)

Revelation
SWP2300A (5-DVD pack)

Ruth
SWP2280A (5-DVD pack)